D1210015

REFLECTIONS

On Praise

REFLECTIONS ON PRAISE

Extracted from WITH THE WORD, published in the USA by Thomas Nelso
Inc., Nashville, Tn.

Published by Nelson Word Ltd 1993.

ISBN 0-85009-227-2 (Australia ISBN 1-86258-143-6)

Reproduced, printed and bound in Great Britain for Nelson Word Ltd., by Isi.
Press, Didcot, Oxon., England.

Photographs used in this book were taken at the following locations:

Front Cover Bay of Islands, New Zealand
Page 8/9 Ilfracombe, Devon
Page 10/11 Vancouver Island
Page 12/13 View across the Rhine, Germany
Page 14/15 Woolstones, Milton Keynes
Page 16/17 Bay of Islands, New Zealand
Page 18/19 Hyde Park, London
Page 20/21 Bancroft, Milton Keynes
Page 22/23 Meopham, Kent
Page 24/25 Bay of Islands, New Zealand
Page 26/27 Copper Mountain, Colorado
Page 28/29 Hyde Park, London

REFLECTIONS

On Praise

WORD PUBLISHING
Nelson Word Ltd
Milton Keynes, England

WORD AUSTRALIA
Kilsyth, Australia

WORD COMMUNICATIONS LTD
Vancouver, B.C., Canada

STRUIK CHRISTIAN BOOKS (PTY LTD)
Cape Town, South Africa

JOINT DISTRIBUTORS SINGAPORE —
ALBY COMMERCIAL ENTERPRISES PTE LTD
and
CAMPUS CRUSADE

CHRISTIAN MARKETING NEW ZEALAND LTD
Havelock North, New Zealand

JENSCO LTD
Hong Kong

SALVATION BOOK CENTRE
Malaysia

WARREN W. WIERSBE

PSALM 29

Praise the LORD, you angels;
  praise the LORD's glory and power.
Praise the LORD for the glory of his name;
  worship the LORD because he is holy.

The LORD's voice is heard over the sea.
  The glorious God thunders;
  the LORD thunders over the ocean.
The LORD's voice is powerful;
  the LORD's voice is majestic.
The LORD's voice breaks the trees;
  the LORD breaks the cedars of Lebanon.

He makes the land of Lebanon dance like
    a calf
  and Mount Hermon jump like a baby bull.
The LORD's voice makes the lightning flash.
The LORD's voice shakes the desert;
  the LORD shakes the Desert of Kadesh.
The LORD's voice shakes the oaks
  and strips the leaves off the trees.
In his Temple everyone says, "Glory to God!"

The LORD controls the flood.
  The LORD will be King for ever.
The LORD gives strength to his people;
  the LORD blesses his people with peace.

Praise before the storm (1–2). David called on the angels in heaven to ascribe praise to God. You never know when a storm is coming, so be sure you are worshipping Him and giving Him all the glory. The greatest beauty of all is the beauty of holiness, and it comes from worshipping the Lord.

Power in the storm (3–9). First the thunder rolled over the Mediterranean Sea. Then the storm broke and moved across the land. Seven times the storm is called "the voice of the LORD". (See Rev. 10:3–4.) What power there is in a storm! Even the angels shout, "Glory!" as they watch it!

Peace after the storm (10–11). David may have seen a rainbow and remembered God's promise given after the Flood (Gen. 9:8–17). God sat as King at the Flood, and He is still King! No storm is greater than God. If you trust Him, the storm will bring glory to God. If life is stormy just now, worship Him and wait on Him. The storm will pass, and He will give you peace.

"God Moves in a Mysterious Way"

God moves in a mysterious way, His wonders to perform.
He plants His footsteps in the sea, and rides upon the storm.
Ye fearful saints, fresh courage take; the clouds ye so much dread
Are big with mercy, and shall break
With blessing on your head.

William Cowper

PSALM 98

Sing to the LORD a new song,
because he has done miracles.
By his right hand and holy arm
he has won the victory.
The LORD has made known his power to save;
he has shown the other nations his victory for his people.
He has remembered his love
and his loyalty to the people of Israel.
All the ends of the earth have seen
God's power to save.

Shout with joy to the LORD, all the earth;
burst into songs and make music.
Make music to the LORD with harps,
with harps and the sound of singing.
Blow the trumpets and the sheep's horns;
shout for joy to the LORD the King.

Let the sea and everything in it shout;
let the world and everyone in it sing.
Let the rivers clap their hands;
let the mountains sing together for joy.
Let them sing before the LORD,
because he is coming to judge the world.
He will judge the world fairly;
he will judge the peoples with fairness.

Why should we praise the Lord? Because of His redemption (v. 1), the revelation of His righteousness (v. 2), and the remembrance of His mercy (v. 3). That should keep you busy singing His praises for a long time!

How should we praise the Lord? With a joyful shout and song (v. 4), and with musical instruments skilfully played to please Him (vv. 5–6). Let voices and instruments join in praising the Lord! Not religious entertainment but the joyful expression of praise to God.

Who should praise the Lord? Everybody in the world—and all the world of nature (vv. 7–9). The anticipation of His coming excites creation, and you should be a part of their excitement.

Joy to the world—the Lord has come!

A New Song

The psalmist often exhorts us to "sing a new song" (Pss. 33:3; 40:3; 96:1; 98:1; 144:9; 149:1). The word translated "new" means "fresh, new in quality". The song may be an old one, but our growth in the Lord and our new experiences of His grace enable us to sing an old song with fresh new meaning and blessing. This explains why the Lord allows us to go through trials. He is tuning us up to praise Him in a new way!

PSALM 147

(verses 1–14)

Praise the LORD!

It is good to sing praises to our God;
it is good and pleasant to praise him.

The LORD rebuilds Jerusalem;
he brings back the captured Israelites.
He heals the broken-hearted
and bandages their wounds.

He counts the stars
and names each one.
Our Lord is great and very powerful.
There is no limit to what he knows.
The LORD defends the humble,
but he throws the wicked to the ground.

Sing praises to the LORD;
praise our God with harps.
He fills the sky with clouds
and sends rain to the earth
and makes grass grow on the hills.
He gives food to cattle
and to the little birds that call.

He does not enjoy the strength of a horse
or the strength of a man.
The LORD is pleased with those who
respect him,
with those who trust his love.

Jerusalem, praise the LORD;
Jerusalem, praise your God.
He makes your city gates strong
and blesses your children inside.
He brings peace to your country
and fills you with the finest grain.

Praising the Lord is the highest exercise of your faculties. He is worthy of praise, and you should praise Him whether or not you think your praise is accomplishing anything in your life. However, there are some blessings that come to those who worship Him in truth.

Praise brings spiritual beauty to God's people (v. 1; Pss. 27:4, 29:2; 149:4). It builds His work and unifies His people (v. 2). It heals the inner person (v. 3) and lifts the fallen (v. 6). Praise is good medicine!

Praise makes God's world real and personal to you (vv. 7–9, 15–18), even the storms; and it is great protection against the enemy (vv. 12–14). Praise pleases the Lord and enables Him to work in your life (vv. 10–11).

PSALM 148

Praise the LORD!

Praise the LORD from the skies.
Praise him high above the earth.
Praise him, all you angels.
Praise him, all you armies of heaven.
Praise him, sun and moon.
Praise him, all you shining stars.
Praise him, highest heavens
and you waters above the sky.
Let them praise the LORD,
because they were created by his command.
He put them in place for ever and ever;
he made a law that will never change.

Praise the LORD from the earth,
you large sea animals and all the oceans,
lightning and hail, snow and mist
and stormy winds that obey him,
mountains and all hills,
fruit trees and all cedars,
wild animals and all cattle,
crawling animals and birds,
kings of the earth and all nations,
princes and all rulers of the earth,
young men and women,
old people and children.

Praise the LORD,
because he alone is great.
He is more wonderful than heaven and earth.
God has given his people a king.
He should be praised by all who belong to him;
he should be praised by the Israelites, the people closest to his heart.

Praise the LORD!

When it comes to praising the Lord, the psalmist will not permit anyone or anything in all creation to escape.

The heavens **(1–6). He starts with the angels, then summons the heavenly bodies, and even includes the clouds! God created them, established them, and controls them. They should praise Him—and they do!**

The earth **(7–10). Whether the depths of the sea or the heights of the mountains, the winds or the fruitful trees, all should praise the Lord—and they do! When the weather is bad, it is good to know that even the storms fulfil God's Word (v. 8).**

Mankind **(11–14). Made in God's image, men and women have more reason to praise God than does any other thing in creation. And when you have been saved by God's grace, your motive is even greater. Praise the Lord!**

PSALM 146

Praise the LORD!
My whole being, praise the LORD.
I will praise the LORD all my life;
I will sing praises to my God as long as I live.

Do not put your trust in princes
or other people, who cannot save you.
When people die, they are buried.
Then all of their plans come to an end.

Happy are those who are helped by the God of Jacob.
Their hope is in the LORD their God.
He made heaven and earth,
the sea and everything in it.
He remains loyal for ever.
He does what is fair for those who have been wronged.
He gives food to the hungry.
The LORD sets the prisoners free.
The LORD gives sight to the blind.
The LORD lifts up people who are in trouble.
The LORD loves those who do right.
The LORD protects the foreigners.
He defends the orphans and widows,
but he blocks the way of the wicked.

The LORD will be King for ever.
Jerusalem, your God is everlasting.

Praise the LORD!

The hymn "Old Hundredth" ("All People That on Earth Do Dwell") is based on this psalm, as is the familiar "Doxology". Thanking the Lord is something we must do with our lives as well as with our lips. How shall we do it?

By serving (2). "Enter to worship—depart to serve" should be written clearly above the door to the church sanctuary. Too many people serve themselves and not the Lord, and too often we do not serve the Lord "with gladness". The Lord loves a cheerful servant.

By submitting (3). As creatures, we submit to the Creator who made us. As sheep, we submit to the Shepherd who died for us and now leads us in His paths. He not only made us, but *He is making us* as we yield to Him (Eph. 2:10). Submission means fulfilment.

By sacrificing (4–5). As priests, we are privileged to offer spiritual sacrifices to the Lord (1 Pet. 2:5). They include our songs of praise (Heb. 13:15), good works (Heb. 13:16), and material gifts (Phil. 4:15–18). Because of who He is (v. 5) and what He does for us, He is certainly worthy of our joyful thanks.

PSALM 145

(verses 4–21)

Parents will tell their children what you
have done.
They will retell your mighty acts,
wonderful majesty and glory.
And I will think about your miracles.
They will tell about the amazing things you do,
and I will tell how great you are.
They will remember your great goodness
and will sing about your fairness.

The LORD is kind and shows mercy.
He does not become angry quickly but is full
of love.
The LORD is good to everyone;
he is merciful to all he has made.
LORD, everything you have made will praise you;
those who belong to you will bless you.
They will tell about the glory of your kingdom
and will speak about your power.
Then everyone will know the mighty things
you do
and the glory and majesty of your kingdom.
Your kingdom will go on and on,
and you will rule for ever.

The LORD will keep all his promises;
he is loyal to all he has made.
The LORD helps those who have been defeated
and takes care of those who are in trouble.
All living things look to you for food,
and you give it to them at the right time.
You open your hand,
and you satisfy all living things.

Everything the LORD does is right.
He is loyal to all he has made.
The LORD is close to everyone who prays to him,
to all who truly pray to him.
He gives those who respect him what they want.
He listens when they cry, and he saves them.
The LORD protects everyone who loves him,
but he will destroy the wicked.
I will praise the LORD.
Let everyone praise his holy name for ever.

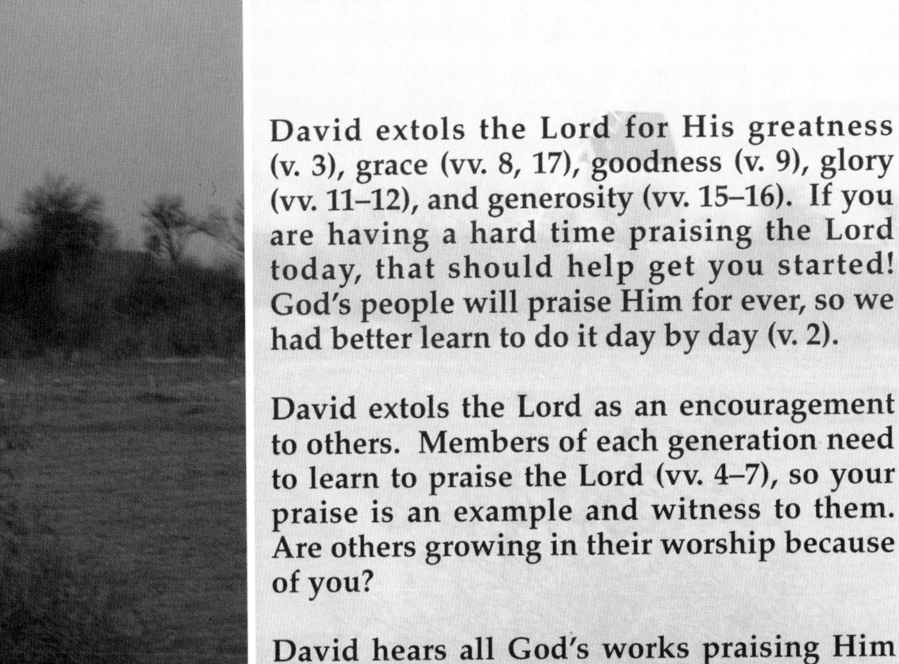

David extols the Lord for His greatness (v. 3), grace (vv. 8, 17), goodness (v. 9), glory (vv. 11–12), and generosity (vv. 15–16). If you are having a hard time praising the Lord today, that should help get you started! God's people will praise Him for ever, so we had better learn to do it day by day (v. 2).

David extols the Lord as an encouragement to others. Members of each generation need to learn to praise the Lord (vv. 4–7), so your praise is an example and witness to them. Are others growing in their worship because of you?

David hears all God's works praising Him (v. 10). Nature takes on new meaning and new beauty when you realise this (Ps. 19:1–6).

When you live a life of praise, you have the Lord's help in every situation. If you stumble, He helps you up (v. 14). If you are hungry, He feeds you (vv. 15–16). If you call, He draws near (v. 18). No wonder David blessed the Lord so much!

PSALM 144

Praise the LORD, my Rock,
who trains me for war,
who trains me for battle.
He protects me like a fortified city, and
he loves me.
He is my defender and my Saviour,
my shield and my protection.
He helps me keep my people under control.

LORD, why are people important to you?
Why do you even think about human beings?
People are like a breath;
their lives are like passing shadows.

LORD, tear open the sky and come down.
Touch the mountains so they will smoke.
Send the lightning and scatter my enemies.
Shoot your arrows and force them away.
Reach down from above.
Save me and rescue me out of this sea of
enemies,
from these foreigners.
They are liars;
they are dishonest.

God, I will sing a new song to you;
I will play to you on the ten-stringed harp.
You give victory to kings.
You save your servant David from cruel swords.

Save me, rescue me from these foreigners.
They are liars; they are dishonest.
Let our sons in their youth
grow like plants.
Let our daughters be
like the decorated stones in the Temple.
Let our barns be filled
with crops of all kinds.
Let our sheep in the fields have
thousands and tens of thousands of lambs.
Let our cattle be strong.
Let no one break in.
Let there be no war,
no screams in our streets.

This is another battle song to help you in your spiritual warfare.

Let God train you *before the battle* (vv. 1–4). In yourself, you are nothing, but God loves you and equips you for what lies ahead. God does not always explain how He prepares you, so accept His disciplines by faith. David fought a lion and a bear before God let him fight a giant. Each morning, put on the whole armour of God and be ready for the trumpet call (Eph. 6:10–18).

Let God help you *in the battle* (vv. 5–8). God's hand is there to strengthen and deliver you, so do not be afraid to engage the enemy. You are fighting the Lord's battles; He will not abandon you (2 Chron. 20:14–19).

Sing God's praises *after the battle* (vv. 9–15). Thank Him for all He has done for you personally (vv. 9–11), for your family (v. 12), and for your nation (vv. 13–15).

PSALM 92

(verses 1–9)

It is good to praise you, LORD,
to sing praises to God Most High.
It is good to tell of your love in the morning
and of your loyalty at night.
It is good to praise you with the ten-stringed lyre
and with the soft-sounding harp.

LORD, you have made me happy by what you have done;
I will sing for joy about what your hands have done.
LORD, you have done such great things!
How deep are your thoughts!
Stupid people don't know these things,
and fools don't understand.
Wicked people grow like the grass.
Evil people seem to do well,
but they will be destroyed for ever.

But, LORD, you will be honoured for ever.

LORD, surely your enemies,
surely your enemies will be destroyed,
and all who do evil will be scattered.

It is good to thank the Lord *for every day He gives you* (vv. 1–4). As the day begins, you can look ahead by faith and praise Him for His loving-kindness. As the day ends, you can look back and praise Him for His faithfulness.

It is good to thank the Lord *that you are part of what is eternal* (vv. 5–9). You cannot understand eternity, but you can have eternal life through faith in Christ; and you can live for what is eternal (1 John 2:17). Ponder 1 Corinthians 15:58.

PSALM 118

(verses 1–16)

Thank the LORD because he is good.
His love continues for ever.

Let the people of Israel say,
"His love continues for ever."
Let the family of Aaron say,
"His love continues for ever."
Let those who respect the LORD say,
"His love continues for ever."
I was in trouble, so I called to the LORD.
The LORD answered me and set me free.
I will not be afraid, because the LORD is with me.
People can't do anything to me.
The LORD is with me to help me,
so I will see my enemies defeated.

It is better to trust the LORD
than to trust people.
It is better to trust the LORD
than to trust princes.

All the nations surrounded me,
but I defeated them in the name of the LORD.
They surrounded me on every side,
but with the LORD's power I defeated them.
They surrounded me like a swarm of bees,
but they died as quickly as thorns burn.
By the LORD's power, I defeated them.

They chased me until I was almost defeated,
but the LORD helped me.
The LORD gives me strength and a song.
He has saved me.

Shouts of joy and victory
come from the tents of those who do right:
"The LORD has done powerful things."
The power of the LORD has won the victory;
with his power the LORD has done mighty things.

The Jewish people sing Psalms 113 to 118 at Passover, so this is one of the songs that Jesus sang before He went to the Garden to pray (Matt. 26:30). If you knew you were going to be executed unjustly, would you be able to sing praises to the Lord?

This is also a messianic psalm. The crowds shouted verses 25–26 as Jesus rode into Jerusalem on Palm Sunday (Matt. 21:9), and Jesus quoted verses 22–23 in His debate with the religious leaders (Matt. 21:33–46).

But it is also a song of praise, thanking God for deliverance from a difficult situation (vv. 10–14). The name of the Lord (vv. 10–12) and the hand of the Lord (vv. 15–16) can give you the victory you need. When you are hemmed in by the enemy (vv. 10–12), cry out to God and He will put you into "a broad place" (v. 5). He will open the gates for you and give you new freedom (vv. 19–20).

Claim verse 24 for every day that you live.

A Song of Faith

"The LORD is my strength and song, and He has become my salvation" (Ps. 118:14).

PSALM 150

Praise the Lord!

Praise God in his Temple;
praise him in his mighty heaven.
Praise him for his strength;
praise him for his greatness.
Praise him with trumpet blasts;
praise him with harps and lyres.
Praise him with tambourines and dancing;
praise him with stringed instruments and flutes.
Praise him with loud cymbals;
praise him with crashing cymbals.

Let everything that breathes praise the Lord.

Praise the Lord!

It is only right that the closing song in the Hebrew hymnal be an invitation to praise the Lord. The word *praise* is used thirteen times here.

Where should we praise Him? Locally and universally, in the temple and in the vast heavens (v. 1). In other words, wherever you are, praise the Lord!

Why should we praise Him? Because of what He does and who He is (v. 2). The better you know God's character and works, the more you will praise Him and the more you will enjoy praising Him.

How should we praise Him? With voices and instruments, including the cymbals, and with our bodies expressing the joy we feel within (vv. 3–5). The whole person should be one living sacrifice that praises the Lord.

Who should praise Him? "Everything that has breath" (v. 6). But things that do not have breath praise Him (Ps. 148:7–9), so we have even more reason to do so! Our breath comes from Him (Acts 17:25), so we ought to use it to praise His name. Breath is the weakest thing we have, but we can devote it to the highest service, praising the Lord.